Drive your Business

with Management and Certainty

Peter H. Antoniou, DBA
Dong Joon Park, Ph. D.

Drive your Business

with Management and Certainty

Peter H. Antoniou, DBA
Dong Joon Park, Ph. D.

ESPRO Inc.

Drive your Business

with Management and Certainty

Peter H. Antoniou, DBA
Dong Joon Park, Ph. D.

Published by ESPRO Inc., California, U.S.

ISBN-13: 978-1492900870

ISBN-10: 1492900877

Printed in the United States of America

DEDICATION

To Nancy and Jessie,
who stand next to us tall and strong

Table of Contents

Preface

This book is part of a series exploring the elements and the relationships between strategy and operations. It sheds light on management's operations in its totality in order to function with more clarity in their actions.

Each book highlights one topic area while it brings the rest of the components in an illustrative format rather than in depth.

It includes tools as well as ways to make strategy and operations work in tandem in order to attain best results in organizations.

The topics at hand are complex. However, the series is written in an easy way so that one can deal and relate to the topics in a non threatening way.

We welcome your thoughts and comments.

Peter H. Antoniou, DBA
Dong Joon Park, Ph. D.

Drive Your Business with Management and Certainty

Drive Your Business with Management and Certainty

Introduction

One of our clients wanted to talk about how to succeed in his business. The inquiry came because he wanted to find out how to move to the next level; how he can move forward as a business. Most of all, he was worried about all the uncertainty and complexity in the market and how he can put all of these concerns into perspective.

Since he was in manufacturing, we knew that he would relate to things better by illustrating the process like some kind of mechanical apparatus. So, we picked up the car as a conceptual illustrative tool of business reality for ease of understanding and concept presentation. This sort of arbitrary selection of the analogy of using an automobile as an example, can not be used as a generalization. However, it might be 'useful' to catch the key concepts and factors which we need to make use in the actual business reality. We use the components of a car as the metaphor to illustrate the relationships that exist in a business and how to make sense of things which seemingly do not have any relations to each other.

All parts are interrelated and play a significant role in the functionality of a car and how it works. In the same way, every component of a business, organization and/or enterprise, is designed and operating in a highly complex interrelated setting. Of course, one can do without some parts, while another might have a strip down version or a supped up one, while others can tolerate some inefficiencies or little scratches on the 'bumper'.

In addition, there a lot more that needs to be taken into consideration; the driver, the type of car, the condition of the road, etc., but all of these are part of the discussion and exploration of the concepts.

All lead into trying to make sense out of concepts, which are related, but yet independent and to bring some certainty into uncertain conditions and circumstances.

This book is part of a series whereby each book focuses on one component of a car, or a component of a business.

While this book alludes to the other components, this book of the series goes much deeper in the strategy and operations of an organization; the engine part. In the meantime, it highlights the rest of the car or business areas.

We wanted to make this book series easy to read and to relate, in order to catch the attention of all those who need to put things into perspective and connect all elements of strategy and business together; to go from simple to more complex in an easy presentation way.

This book is intended for all those who are interested in the topic area of strategy and business. We are trying to make uncertain things certain, and complex ones less threatening. By no means the topics are not important or impactful. On the contrary, they are significant, complex, interdependent but manageable.

Drive Your Business with Management and Certainty

1

Setting the Stage

There is massive amount of literature on strategy, business and management with tremendous contribution on theories, concepts and approaches as to how things should take place. Literature is full of prescriptions as to 'how to' and 'what to' do.

The material is complicated, do not underestimate that. However, in looking at each one of its parts it does make sense as to what is the part and how it relates to every other.

In order to simplify the presentation of the concepts we use the metaphor of a car and its components. The need to demonstrate the concepts and relationships via an illustration was developed as part of a presentation we gave to one of our clients. It helped present 'where we go next' and how does each part of the operation is related and affected.

So, we use the analogy of a car. The car consists of multiple sub components, each having its own technological speed. It is controlled by the one entity, the driver (CEO) predominantly, and passengers (corporate officers and staff), while influenced by the car owners (BOD). It also has a set of dashboard control mechanisms to assess how the car is operating. It has gears, to help its speed and operational swiftness, an engine compartment (which few see but all depend on) and of course brand and make which equates to the organization's marketing persona in the publics' eyes.

All of these components are interconnected to the ultimate performance of the car.

Any business is like a type of an automobile. It can be classified as a passenger car, light truck, van, dump truck or an 18 wheeler. Within each category there are variants; like in the passenger car category there are compact cards, 4-door sedans, luxury, 2-door, sports or smart cars just to name a few. All organizations can be classified in any of these 'sizes' and types which are based on industry and size potential.

Source: http://www.ford.com/

Source: http://www.chevrolet.com/

It all depends on what the driver/entrepreneur wants to achieve and how large he/she wants the vehicle to become. This is based on the mission and vision of the entrepreneur and that of the board of directors.

9

We can even make the example a little more graphic by introducing motorcycles as part of the illustration since there are one man operations. These are literally the mom and pop operations. They fit in the illustration since they depict the loneliness of the single operator.

One can start with a motorcycle and 'upgrade' to a car (hire more people) and then get to the next size up, or to get a truck based on the type of industry and size of business that wants to have or to become.

Businesses are categorized as small businesses (SBA's), medium and large; the same as automobiles. However, all vehicles have some things in common: all have drivers, all have engines, all have passengers, all have wheels and all are designed for different terrains. This is the premise that we use to illustrate the power of strategy and management in any business.

By the way, as we present things, we want to make it very clear that there is no difference whether an organization is designated for profit, or non-profit ones. There is absolutely no difference between them when it comes to developing strategy and needed outcomes. The only difference between the two is that the non-profit organizations have a different tax liability where they are allowed to retain their profits in order to reinvest them back into the business. By no means, however, this is a 'ticket' for a non- profit organization to be inefficient or ineffective in its operations. They follow exactly the same rules as the for profit ones in regards to operations and profitability.

The same applies for governmental organizations, schools, health organizations and all other environment serving organizations. All have the same goal: to serve the needs of the external environment, or they will go out of business. Case in point, stellar organizations which folded over times are RCA, Builder's Emporium and KODAC, to name a few.

So, let's put the car components into perspective then.

We have the car itself, the driver, the owner(s), passengers, what is under the hood, the engine, engine size, belt system, gears/transmission, tires, trunk, windshield. Most of all we look at the car itself, its make, condition and the driver. How different is it with a business?

When we look at the:

> car = company itself

> type/make/model = the industry and the position in the market in regards to competition

condition = financial health, wealth and operational condition of the organization, whether clean, dirty, or scratched

driver = CEO

owner(s) = board of directors

passengers = corporate officers and staff

engine size/ cylinders = size of the organization

belt system = relationships between strategy, management and operation

gears/transmission = ways to change size, speed / shift in management, organizational structure, design operation and direction

tires = it is the direct contact with clients, dealing with operation

trunk = spared resources in case of emergency, (tire, tools) signifying the depth of the organization, as well as other stuff we carry that we hardly use and we have forgotten about

windshield = the organization's view of the future

Drive Your Business with Management and Certainty

The clear understanding each of these parts helps to creating a certainty in setting the course of actions for an organization.

So, let's start exploring the car...

Drive Your Business with Management and Certainty

2

Car: The Company itself

When we look at a car on the road we immediately classify it in various categories depending on its size, make, style, color and usage.

It can be small compact, mid size, luxury sedan, sports car, or truck, van, bus or an 18 wheeler. It is exactly the

Drive Your Business with Management and Certainty

same in business; Businesses can be classified as small businesses (SBAs), small and medium enterprises (SMEs), or conglomerates. They vary in legal structure of that of a proprietorship, partnership or corporation based on the intent of the set up and the advantages that one tries to gain based each state's tax system.

They vary in complexity, size and resources. They have different organization structure from simple to multidivisional and they cover the domestic and international markets.

The fact that it is a car, it distinguishes from other moving vehicles, namely, motorcycles, trucks, boats and planes as means of possible transportation. All of which provide means of motorized transportation.

We also need to assess the terrain as the whether a boat could be most appropriate. Though there are some amphibious cars these are the ones that are good as hybrids. You get the point; while a car is a means of transportation of a certain type, an organization, in parallel, is a means of satisfying a particular need in a certain geographical area for a specified type of a client, by utilizing a distinct distribution channel.

Now like cars one can use it for one application or another. You might use it to move your dresser to your new house or apartment, but it is not designed for that unless you make certain modifications to your car. The same in an organization, you can serve more than one type of a client, or use more than one distribution channel. If it is done on an on-going basis you might need to change the organization's structure to support the new function. Even though it might be 'good enough' for a couple of times or for the short run, it does not serve well what needs to happen in a consistent basis in the long run.

This leads us to the different types and models of cars.

Drive Your Business with Management and Certainty

Drive Your Business with Management and Certainty

3

Type/make/model: the industry and the type of business necessary

The type, make and model of a car is the indication as to the type of vehicle that is needed based on the purpose and need. It can be a motorcycle, car, van, bus or truck whichever is appropriate for the purpose that is fulfilling.

Drive Your Business with Management and Certainty

The mission and vision is articulated prior to buying a car. The same applies in business. First you decide what you want to do and then you plan, allocate resources and get it. Based on the articulated vision you buy the car that best fits your needs. If it is for light transport, you might want to get a light truck, if it is to transport people, you might want to get a sedan (taxi), or a van, or a bus for even more people. If it is to transport cargo you might need to get a trailer truck, or a dump truck.

This would affect the size of the business that you need to have. In some businesses one needs to have critical mass in order to conduct business, i.e. starting a bank, or a rental car company.

The same applies if you operate in the service industry, or in construction, or transportation. Each necessitates a different type of structure size and support.

This is the realization that 'there are different horses for different courses'. In other words one has to build an organization which would function successfully in one type of an industry, but not necessarily in another.

There is a special usage for a race car, a different for a utility vehicle and yet another for a bus. Yes, there can be some overlap between types, makes and models but in the most cases one vehicle can not be fully utilized in

Drive Your Business with Management and Certainty

two industries. The same applies in business. Organizations are designed to serve one industry and sometimes overlap another. It is based on the customer type that they try to follow and satisfy. Look at banks for instance; there are some which are predominantly retail ones and others which are retail and investment and commercial ones. All types are quite successful in their own regard.

Like with any car types and their classification, in one's mind, what comes next is rivalry. First there is rivalry between any and all vehicles which occupy space in a motorway and then there is direct completion between the same type of cars. So, there is rivalry between the industry sectors and there is direct competition between the players within any given industry. So, here we need to talk about competition, competitive forces assessment and the works.

Like a car, when one looks at its make and model, is positively or negatively predisposed. The industry, market and conditions directly affect its image. For instance, dealing with diamonds or luxury items it has a different image than dealing with office or household supplies. Not only there is difference in profit margins, but there is difference in expectation of treatment. The same applies in business: the treatment is different at

Tiffany's or Bloomindales's vs. Office Depot or Target. There are perceived differences and expectations between a Rolls Royce or a Cadillac and a Toyota or a Buick.

But more on these come a little later.

4

Condition: Financial Health, Wealth and Operational Condition of the Organization

Here we assess the overall health of the organization. It ranges from financial to operational in addition to the organization's systems which are in place.

While one has a certain type or a model of a car, it does not mean that 'it is treated' very well. How many times you saw a Benz or a Caddie that was dirty and not kept up and you were wondered whether the driver was doing justice to the car? By the way, when one buys a Rolls Royce, the new buyer signs an agreement with the dealer that the driver will not drive the car if or when it gets scratched or damaged since it does not reflect well to the image of Rolls Royce on the street. At the same time, when a Rolls breaks down, a white covered tow truck shows up, loads it in the back and rolls down the door. No Rolls can be seen being towed! It is part of the image.

The same with a Ferrari; one can not buy a new one as a first time buyer. Even if you had the money to buy it you have to buy a used one first to ensure that you know "how to drive" and treat the car properly. After one year you can buy a new one.

So, in addition to the outside condition of the car, its wax job, scratches and the works, the driver is interested in making sure that the car operates in its maximum capacity at all times.

Thus, we use instruments to assess how the car is run. The same in an organization; we use tools to interpret signals as to how the organization is doing. Some of these criteria are subjective and some are objective, like in a car. A gauge is subjective, but the feel as to how the car drives is subjective.

The Balance Scorecard is one of the tools which is used to assessing how an organization fares in 'a quick a dirty' look. It incorporates a wide range of tools forcing a more objective look rather than a subjective one.

In addition to the measure itself, there is comparison to the industry averages to find out how well the organization is doing in comparison to its peers.

Quarterly financials, performance indicators and price to earnings (P/E) ratios along with shareholder value, are key into finding out how an organization is doing.

Notice that we introduced the shareholder value and stock value as additional indicators. These are affected based as to whether your car is cleaned and waxed or dirty and scratched

Marketing, and in particular public relations, plays a pivotal role on the organization's image to the publics. How well a car is waxed and kept up gives a completely different image and perspective. It indicates that it is cared for and then has more value. Think of all the things that you do when you are about to sell your car ... you make it look much cleaner so to look more cared for than when you drive it regularly.

Marketing helps mold as to how an organization is perceived in the eyes of the customer while continuously fostering the company's image.

There are a series of tools and actions that are to be explored in turn to make this happen.

Drive Your Business with Management and Certainty

5

Driver: CEO

Probably the most important part in the organization is the role of the CEO. The heart and soul of the organization.

Drive Your Business with Management and Certainty

The CEO is the one who puts the key in the ignition and starts the car. It is the driver who decides on the direction, the one who motivates and overseas all about the organization.

The drive is the one who articulates the vision and the mission of the organization. Is the main communicator of the organization and the one in the spot light. Is the one all talk about and the one in the driver's seat. You look at the driver of car next to you when stopped at a traffic light to size up the driver next to you and to figure out the potential to overpass him/her...

The CEO's individual's motivation, risk propensity, skill level, ability to interpret incomplete information and make sense out of them as well as his/her personality are key components of how the organization will run. Exactly the same with the car driver. The driver is the key as to how the car is driven and how it will operate; whether on its maximum capacity, or coasting. How many times you have seen on the road a nice powerful car and it ridden rather meekly and you said to yourself 'what a shame...'.

As to the driver's skills, one can see them in action not only in perfect weather conditions, but when there is slit, rain, or other adverse conditions. This is when the skills of the driver, CEO, are truly tested. It is when there is a need for tough decisions and particularly when there is a need for change in the organization's course.

Obviously one needs a different driver based on the type of vehicle he/she is to operate. One needs a different license for a moped, motorcycle, passenger car and another if it is to drive a bus or a truck. The same in business; the CEO needs to have the training for the size of an organization, the complexity of environment and the potential terrain in order to be successful.

The CEO is the one who will put emphasis on growth, concentrate in operating turnaround, or take full advantage of the organization's efficiencies.

The CEO is the one to change gears, or to put the car on overdrive based on internal and external forces. Is the one who takes the glory and deals with accusations at all times.

There are a number of tools that a driver uses when riding a car. A driver uses the dashboard instruments to make sense as to how the car is operating. Mind you, the driver does not need all information, but the critical ones and even the summary of those. In looking at a car's dashboard one can only see a small number of dials about the car's operation. They are usually instruments for engine temperature, gasoline and oil levels as well speedometer, odometer and tachometer.

These by no means interpret all the subcomponents of the operation of a car. They are good indicators as to how the car appears to operate as a whole. The same applies in business; the CEO might use a quick and dirty interpretation as to how the company is doing by looking at operating expenses, income, expenses, burn rate (how much we spend on a monthly basis), and at sales figures, purchase orders (POs), ROI, and stock price.

The collection and summation of these numbers is critical and take a tremendous amount of time and effort to ensure accuracy since so much is riding on the interpretation. It is the same as to your looking at the gasoline gauge; you want it be accurate enough so you know how far you can travel. If there is a mistake you might run out of gas and get stuck on the side of the road.

In a car you are also looking at the speedometer; it is the same as the sales numbers in the organization. You want to know what Purchase Orders (POs) you have booked for the quarter and thus, the expected outcomes.

These give you a fast interpretation in monitoring the conditions of the car. The same applies in organizations; you use a set of tools to monitor performance.

Drive Your Business with Management and Certainty

6

Owner(s): Board of Directors

While the driver is the one who maneuvers the car, the registered owner might be someone else. This is when your spouse likes your car more than hers, or your child drives your car. The car is yours but the driver is another.

It is the same in an organization. If the organization is public, the ownership representation lies with the Board of Directors (BOD). If the company is private then the role of the BOD is more of an advisory one serving as an overseer of the company to offer advise to the CEO and major owners.

In a public company, the ownership is shared by the shareholders who can be investors (private and/or institutional), individuals (associated or not with the company), other companies, and the company itself.

Now you see the conflict already...; some might be interested in the growth of the stock value, others are looking for a faster ROI of their investment while some others are interested in dividend payout.

The role of the BOD is to represent the interests of the owners (in a public company). So the BOD hires a CEO to act on their behalf to implement and achieve what the owners want.

Table 1 introduces the BOD's functions in relation to corporate governance.

While the Board is responsible for the big picture focusing on the long run, the CEO is responsible for the day to day operation ensuring implementation of the 'long run'.

In addition, the CEO is the one who calibrates the organization's capabilities and introduces new ones to attain future potential opportunities for the organization.

At times the CEO's direction of the future and that of the BOD's are not exactly aligned and problems arise. In private companies that is not much of a problem since the CEO is usually the major owner and can decide what he/she wants despite the views of the Board. But in public companies it can be problematic having a runaway CEO and management team. That is why

Drive Your Business with Management and Certainty

Sharbanes Oxley Act was put in place to control both the CEO and in particular the Board members so that they truly act on behalf of the owners and not being manipulated by the CEO and corporate officers.

	Corporate Governance
Board functions	• Strategic planning • Risk identification and management • Selection, oversight and compensation of senior management • Succession planning • Communication with shareholders • Integrity of financial controls • General legal compliance
References	Canada's Dey report, France Viénot Report, Malaysia's Report on Corporate Governance, Mexico's Code of Corporate Governance, South Africa's King Report, Korean Stock Exchange Code

Source: Holly J. Gregory, "*Overview of Corporate Governance Guidelines and Code of Best Practice in Developing and Emerging Markets,*" Robert A. G. Monks and Nell Minow, Corporate Governance, Blackwell Publishing, 2004, p. 533.

Table 1. Board Responsibilities and Job description

The Board's role and operation differs in other parts of the world. In some, the members serve as active participants to the implementation of the directives and in other countries they are more passive. In some counties the CEO can not be the Chairman of the Board while in others it can.

Regardless, the CEO and the board work closely together with the same goal in mind: the overall success of the organization. The Board and CEO might differ in the interpretation as to how to obtain that, but this is a discussion for late.

7

Passengers: Corporate Officers, Managers and Staff

Passengers are the ones who board the vehicle of the company. They are the so called 'organized personnel'. As we use the analogy of the car, organized personnel directly influences the organization's external environment and its stakeholders alike.

Internal stakeholders are the people who are the employees of the organization and members of the Board of Directors.

Like in a car, each of the internal stakeholders could be seated in the front seat, or in the back, or in the bucket seat if it is a van. However, regardless as to where one sits, each person (of the organized personnel) holds a position:

1. fulfilling the needs of the organization's mission, plans, operation, communication, as well as,

2. being accountable based on the 4 Rs: Responsibility, Roles, Results and Rewards.

The 'seat', position descriptions are illustrated in table 2.

	4Rs			
	Responsibility	Role	Results	Rewards
Mission				
Planning & Execution				
Operational Control				
Communications				

Table 2: Position Description

Each seat has the common and unique mission and 4Rs, which set the fundamental operational activities to each passenger.

Depending on the kind of car there is a distinct difference of the passengers based on composition, cross functional skills responsibilities, skill set, knowledge motivation and tenacity.

Remember, there are different kinds of cars, sizes and for different purposes and terrains necessitating different skill set and composition of the 'organized personnel'.

One example is a military vehicle for the armored forces; the specialized functional solders will be the passengers for the strategic maneuver. In order to achieve business success, every passenger has a responsibility, role and reward commensurate to the 'seat'.

If we change the example from the military to a cargo truck, the passengers' position description would be focusing on the operability and performance.

On another area of the seat arrangement: the closer to the driver, the higher the influence level. The driver (CEO) cannot accomplish everything by him/herself though.

The driver needs to have the input from all the 'passengers' as to what they see, do, and work towards the successful execution of operations.

Each passenger acts as the eyes, ears, mouth and brains of the mission of the organization, the united 'car way'.

Drive Your Business with Management and Certainty

The expectation is that each passenger is active participant of the organization while they are on board.

It might be that a passenger might stay on board for a little bit and then get off, or stay for a long while. The expectation is that as long as one is on board we put all the best possible effort to accomplish the common goal (that of the individual's as well as the organization's). After a while if there is a divergence of goals, a passenger might get off.

Again the expectation is that this is not a taxi ride whereby, as an individual, I don't sit back and the taxi takes me, and I just enjoy the ride without any contribution.

This glimpse of the passengers is explored further in a subsequent publication.

8

Engine Size/Cylinders: Size of the Organization

Engine size refers to the business capability especially for the resource transformation capacity of business processing.

It requires 150 hundred plus sets of dishes at a 100 hundred seats restaurant, whereas 300 hundred plus sets of those at a 200 hundred seats restaurant. As for the Kitchen, it requires same math to set the furnaces, ovens, pots and pans, hotplates and work space to fulfill the size and the request of the menus in accordance to the business size, customer and market competitive environment.

41

The same applies to a car. There are various engine sizes from 2 to 4, 6, 8, or 12 cylinders and more. A different size would give different output in regards to speed, strength, torck, horse power.

A big engine does not always have the best output when it comes to strength. Getting the strength, relative to the scale of economy, the aimed market size, and its future potential should be always kept in mind.

We also need to realize that the belt system plays a significant role in relationship between strategy, management and operation.

The engine oil directly affects how well the operation runs and it directly affects the engine's maintenance.

More specifically on this since it is the center piece of the series. The Business Engine is explored in the subsequent chapters.

9a

The Business Engine

The engine is the heart of a car. It includes a number of contraptions which help propel the car. Any mishap will make it to not go.

Source: http://pretoria.olx.co.za/hyundai-korean-motor-spare-part-in-silverton-pretoria-east-iid-449908942

The business engine reminds the fan/belt system of a car. The relationships of the activities are the same: a system of interdependent components where all parts depend on each other, all parts move separately and in tandem, one wheel (activity) propels the other and the tension changes at all times. Regardless, all parts depend on each other for a successful operation.

The size of the engine itself is not of any consequence for this discussion since the principal is the same regardless of the 'engine's size'. The system is the same. We will talk more about size later.

The fan/belt system - Business Engine is illustrated in figure 1.

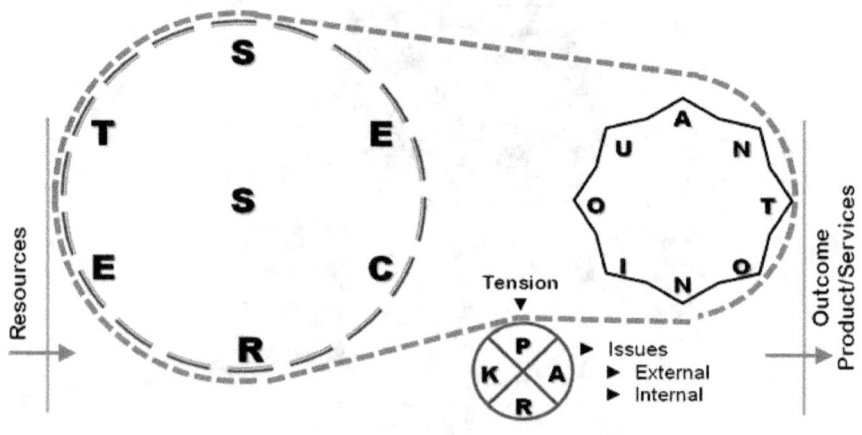

<Peter H. Antoniou and D. J. Park, 2011>

Figure 1: The Business Engine

Drive Your Business with Management and Certainty

Notice that the ignitor (entrepreneurship) along with fuel (which is the mission, profits, will, etc) is not illustrated in this figure.

On the left, the larger wheel, illustrates the *where* the organization is headed, the Direction of the organization. The smaller one on the right illustrates the *how*, Operations/implementation of the organization. The connecting Belt is management and the Tensioner represents the various issues (both internal and external) the organization faces and needs to deal with. We will talk about each of them in greater detail.

This is a live system. Depending on the situation, the wheels turn faster or slower, with more or less tension. The wheels change in size to accommodate changes coming from the Direction wheel as well from the Tensioner. These changes directly affect Operations which would, in turn, alter strategic direction necessitating more 'gears' to the Operation to get what the organization wants to attain. But we are getting ahead of ourselves; let's start from the beginning.

The larger wheel, on the left, (Direction) is comprised of 7 areas (teeth) which grab on the belt (management) to make the Operations wheel turn. These 7 areas are: **S**trategy, **E**nvironment, **C**apability, **R**esources, **E**xecution, **T**actics, **S**uccess (SECRETS).

The smaller wheel (Operations) has 8 teeth which are: **A**pplication, **N**avigation, **T**eamwork, **O**perations, **N**egotiation, **I**mplementation, **O**utcomes, **U**rgency. The Tensioner consists of 4 components. These are: **P**arameters, **A**ccelerators, **R**eactors, and **K**ey Performance Indices.

9b

The Wheels' Sizes

The size of each wheel plays a significant role. The Direction wheel is larger because it drives Operations/implementation and it can make Operations run more efficiently and in the right direction during stable conditions.

The wheels turn in alignment to ensure that there is maximum output at all times. This is what management (Belt) concentrates in.

The size of the Direction wheel changes depending on how turbulent or stable the overall environment/situation is, as well the transformation that takes place in the organization at the time.

Here is what we mean about alignment between wheels. In stable times the Direction wheel is larger because the Direction is established and there are more long range planning issues versus short term (immediate issues/operating concerns) the organization faces. Strategy and overall direction is more of an annual planning process. On the other hand, Operations is the one that takes the brunt in getting things done in the best possible manner, trying to get the maximum efficiencies out of the system. Consequently, in stable times, the Operations wheel is the smaller of the two, working harder and it 'turns' faster.

During turbulent times it is the reverse. There is a significant need in assessing the organization's direction and potentially changing the organization's direction. During turbulent times the Direction wheel is smaller because it is working harder to get things done. The focus in turbulent times is how to be able to address and deal with the direction of the organization and how to survive the next wave of impending changes. The Direction wheel is working harder, turning many more times to get things ready as to what needs to happen.

During transition times, when there is change in the organization, there is a need of change of speed to shift from where we are today to where we want to be. So, we apply different gears to either rev up the engine or to take it to a higher gear, going faster and, thus, expanding the organization's reach. We will introduce the gear changing process, to take us from where we are today to where we want to be, a bit later.

However, at this point let's talk about each of the Direction 'teeth' to understand them more and see their interrelationships before we talk about other engine's parts.

9c

The Direction Wheel

The Direction wheel has 7 components or 'teeth', as shown in repeat figure 1 bellow.

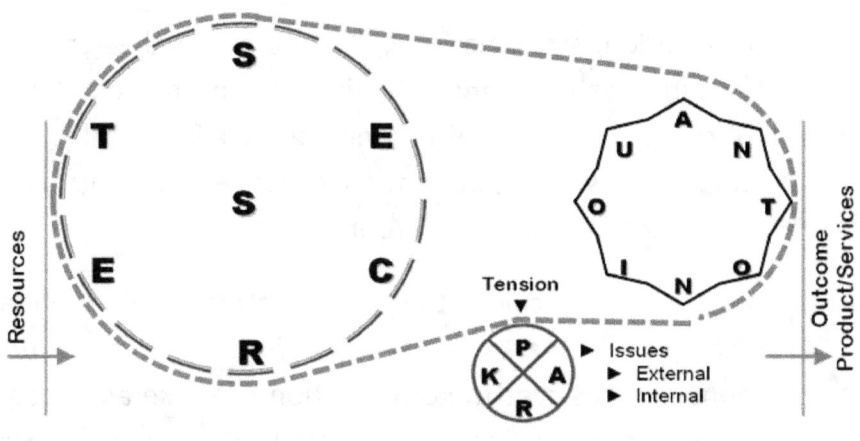

< Peter H. Antoniou and D. J. Park, 2011>

Figure 1: The Business Engine

Drive Your Business with Management and Certainty

Strategy is the approach that the organization adopts to be successful in the future. There are different types of strategies depending on size and scope. There are business level strategies, one for each of the divisions, Strategic Business Units for industry groups, or corporate level strategies for the organization as an overall.

Some of the strategies are generic ones and some are unique. The strategies depend based on whether the aim is to serve 90% of the potential market or the 10% of it.

In addition, strategies vary depending on the types of industry itself, and more significantly on the complexity of the environment of the industry itself. Basically how stable or fast changing is the industry. This brings us to the next component, Environment.

Environment includes the interpretation of all potential changes in the organization's future. It includes opportunities that the organization can take advantage of both from the external and internal environments; threats which are areas of possible negative impact in the industry and consequently the organization, and; trends which are events and changes in the industry and the business area in general which have an upwards or downward trajectory. Trends usually have not materialized (yet) as to their potential outcome and whether they are going to be potential opportunities or threats. They are still in the process of developing.

The external environment indicates new areas that can be exploited as well as areas to look out for. These are not recommended actions other than areas of potential calamity or advantage. All of these impending changes are generated by a multitude of actions ranging from the general environment, including technology changes, legal, political, etc, to industry specific, namely competitors, suppliers, regulators and the works. All these changes are in the form of signals which are sent into the environment for all to see (provided that organizations are able to, having the appropriate tools to collect, analyze and interpret them).

At the same time, any of the actions of any of the players in an industry (introducing a new product, changing pricing strategy, etc) sends a signal to the environment of the change/ position of that particular player. The same applies to any event about anything.

These signals are part of the read-out as to what is happening or what will be happening in the future directly affecting the business engine. Each one of the signals, as soon as it is identified, is classified in a category depending on its speed (how fast is coming towards us), its impact (what affect will it have when it will 'hit'/get to us. Each signal, from then on, is traced, followed and reassessed on an ongoing basis.

The idea is to ensure that each of the signals is followed and projects/ actions are put in place to address what to do about each of the signals identified.

By the way, the very same mechanism is used whether the signal comes from the external or internal environment.

Talking about the internal environment; it includes abilities that the organization has and needs to build to distinguish itself. These could be potential competencies in the market place. These competencies can be based on resources that the organization has, like: contracts, assets, access to distribution channels (to name a few), or abilities of the organization itself like innovation, speed, access to distribution channel, brand name, etc. It also includes the ability of the organization to get things done.

Regardless, the most influential part of the Environment is the external one since it is the indicator as to what is going to be happening in the industry next. Assessment of the external environment is quite important so as to not misinterpret what the industry will be facing in the near and long term future. This way the organization can align itself as to what it needs in preparing for these impending changes.

Going back to the internal environment, we mentioned the abilities of the organization to get things done. This is the organization's Capability.

Capability is the ability of an organization to deal with what needs to happen. It includes both: the abilities of the organization as a system of operations (hardware), as well as the people themselves, their abilities, know-how, skills, ambition, motivation, etc, (software). The combination of the hardware and software of the organization helps to interpret, analyze, design, manage and oversee all what is needed in an organization. The main driver of the organization's Capability design is the CEO. This person is the one who executes the strategic direction set by the Board of Directors and identifies the way to get the best strategy implemented. It is the CEO who commits and builds the resources to get things done in an organization.

Now, in order to make the Capabilities come true the organization utilizes resources. The right selection of resources, their correct build up and their proper application directly influences outcomes.

Resources include all that an organization system has and needs to have to bring to reality what the organization wants to achieve. These include, and are not limited to, having a clear understanding of what 'we really want' and 'what we have at hand' in order to put them in their best utilization. For instance, the appropriate people's skill set, processes, logistics, management quality level, technical skills, money and technology, to name a few.

Resources can be tangible and intangible including patents, contracts, location as well as know-how, reputation in the market as well as and processes and agility of the organization among many others. The major influencer for whatever the organization has or does is management which directly influences the direction and consequently resource determination of the organization.

Think of a car; the type of car, make, size, age, weight tire thread and inflation, etc. plays a significant role to its performance and its ability to 'race' another car at a traffic light. There are tangible components. The driver's skill set, the motivation, mood, as well as vision, passengers' influence on driving style and direction constitute the intangible parts of any organization.

Resources are fostered, cultivated, developed, acquired, outsourced and wasted depending on the situation and the organization.

Resources are the conduit to getting things done leading us to the next component/tooth, Execution.

Execution is getting it done. It is discovering the appropriate direction which will give the organization the highest potential for growth and ability to make a profit or fulfillment of its goal(s) by putting it/them in action. This is committing to the direction that the organization is going to take and utilizing all that it takes to get it done. While Peter Drucker said that management is: "Getting things done through people", execution is getting it done in the most effective and efficient way. In other words doing the right thing and doing it right. This is what separates and distinguishes a stellar organization. It is mustering all the resources available to get the right things done right. This is the tooth that puts the right components in place in getting the right direction of the organization in achieving the organization's goals.

Tactics entail the fine tuning of the strategy and its application in order to give the organization its distinction in the marketplace. Now, this can be messy since one needs to keep a very close eye to monitoring and adjusting accordingly. Tactics are easily reversible and give a temporary advantage to the organization. Nothing permanent. These are quick steps to stay in the forefront in the eyes of the customer and solidify position in the marketplace.

Tactics include price discounts, and posturing in the market place. They are not permanent since the other competitors can match it. Tactics are directly tied with marketing strategies which communicate to the publics where the organization is and what is trying to achieve.

These are tuning your car, putting new tires, washing it and making it run to its best possible shape. Each competitor could get a same advantage quite easily. This is not a permanent but rather a temporary advantage.

While tactics lead to shorter term gains, strategies have longer term impacts. Strategies are more permanent and longer lasting, much more difficult to imitate; like building a new plant (which gives permanent capacity expansion), or entering into a merger agreement, or buying another company, or selling part of operations.

These equate to one buying a car in a different class, which would give a permanent advantage, ie. selling a compact car and buying a luxury or a sports car. One trades to a different set of permanent advantage that the car 'class' provides. The sports car will outperform the compact car under any circumstances due to its design. It provides a permanent advantage, one that can not be duplicated by competition other than buying the same type or model of a car.

Success is set in the center of the wheel since this is the hub and the answer to all of what we are doing. This is where all the measures of achievement come from. It is the most difficult one to deal with since the organization looks at it at all times as measures of survival.

Success is directly juxtaposed in attaining the specific directives of the organization. These directives include (in very broad terms) the organization's goals and objectives, ROI, quarterly returns, as well as new products and presence in markets. These directives are defined by the board of directors and senior management and are closely watched and responded on a quarterly basis through the reported financials.

The organization needs to maintain the hunger for renewal and growth as momentum of survival. Success can be a self fulfilling prophecy which can easily become a demise when unharnessed. We saw the spectrum of

Drive Your Business with Management and Certainty

outcomes in numerous organizations like RCA as an unsuccessful one and IBM at the opposite spectrum.

9d

SECRETS – The Explanation

The SECRETS model was developed when we worked on the research and analysis of executives' success behavior. We found that business executives approach their business execution in two different ways.

One group of executives executes their business under the strategic paradigm approach. This approach matches the elements of Environment to the organization's strategy design supporting by the organization's ability to get things done towards successful implementation. These types of executives work hard in interpreting what the Environment will potentially look like and aligning the appropriate strategy to the impending changes as they interpret them. (This is what IBM did in changing from mainframe computers to an information solution/provider/support services approach).

The other group of executives take operations as a given. They basically try to find out in which other areas they can utilize what they do best. The focus is mainly as to where they can apply what the organization does best. They focus on the daily execution and they do not look at anything else. (This is what Dell has been doing in identifying which other products they can add to their successful model of Just In Time ordering and fantastically efficient operations. By the way they are in the process of redesigning themselves).

The first group we named it the SECS model because it focuses on the three basic elements related with Success: Environment, Capability and Strategy. This approach is based on the typical Strategic Management traditional framework and is illustrated in figure 2.

Figure 2: SECS Model

In the SECS model, Strategy (and planning) is the center of attention. So this can be called strategy-driven management.

The second group focuses more on the existing resources and daily execution as the main driver for success. They respond to each of the issues with the tactical business intelligence. This kind of business approach is comprised of three elements related with Success. These are Responses, Executions and Tactics for Success. So it can be named as RETS model illustrated in figure 3.

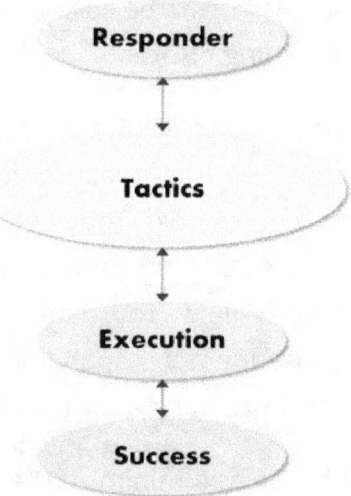

Figure 3: RETS Model

Drive Your Business with Management and Certainty

RETS is based on operational performance. It is focused on the success of execution and operations, so this can be called operation-driven management.

IN both instances the emphasis is on the responder, the person in charge, the CEO, the driver. This would directly influence the resources (and their utilization) that the organization has which would alter the organization's emphasis and direction.

Each of the types has specific strengths and weaknesses. The SECS model might have strategic rationality in designing and implementation for strategic success. But the senior managers might be losing response time in the design and planning efforts.

On the other hand, in the RETS model approach, senior management could be too focused in the execution efforts of current operations. They could have strategic myopia (inability to see far enough into the future). This would cause failure to identify environmental changes and subsequently capability redesign along with new strategic fit to business situations.

Therefore to enhance and minimize the defects of these two heterogeneous models, a new integrated model comprised of the SECS + RETS models was constructed called the SECRETS model. It is illustrated in figure 4.

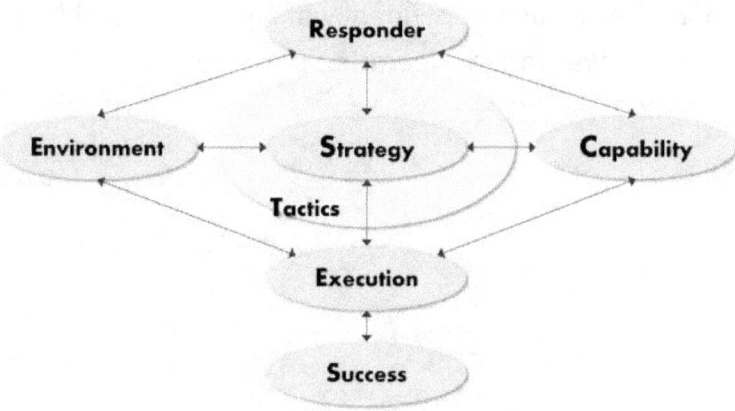

Figure 4: SECRETS Model

Better for our purposes, Success is the center of the Wheel illustrated in figure 5 bellow.

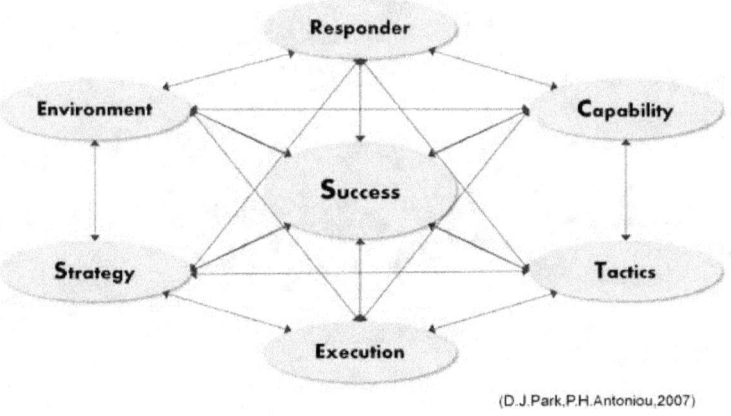

(D.J.Park,P.H.Antoniou,2007)

Figure 5: Conceptual Diagram of the SECRETS Model

Drive Your Business with Management and Certainty

Notice the link and dependency of all of the "teeth" in order to have smooth operation of the wheel.

9e

The Operation Wheel

But let's go back to the business engine morel, figure 1.

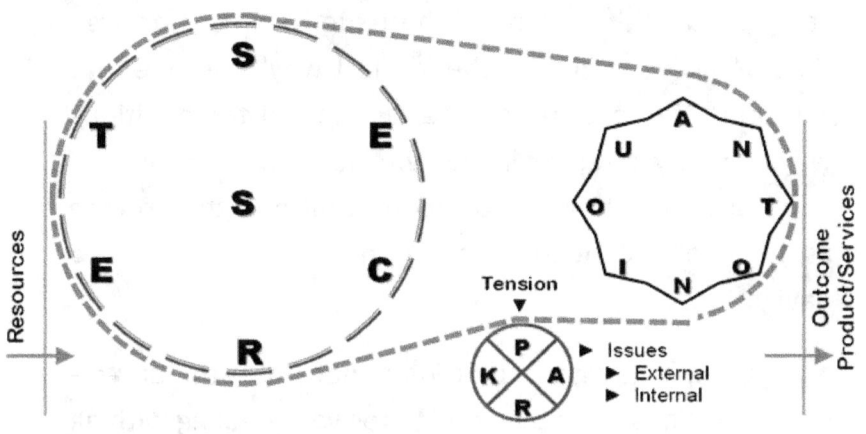

< Peter H. Antoniou and D. J. Park, 2011>

While the wheel on the left is the Direction one (Strategy), the wheel on the right is the Operations one. Similarly, Operations has a number of teeth (components) which help propel (or sometimes slow down) the turning of the apparatus, the organization itself. The teeth in the Operations wheel are: **A**pplication, **N**avigation, **T**eamwork, **O**perations, **N**egotiation, **I**mplementation, **O**utcomes, **U**rgency.

Here is a short introduction of each of the components.

Application deals with the different speeds, approaches, 'the way we do things here', as well as identifying all possible ways to address and solve the '*how* we are going to get things done'. The issue of time, 'the way that we always done it', the 'easiest way', the one that will bring the least resistance, or the most expeditious way, directly affects all that we do. The appropriate application and how we go about it, affects the process as to what we need to get done. This leads us to navigation.

Navigation is going through the minefield of the day-to-day operations. It is the leaping forward dealing with all that it takes to ensure that all gets done in the most efficient and effective way. It includes the measuring and comparing as to whether we have achieved the goals for the shift/day/week/month/quarter. It is what happens on the ground floor on a daily basis, to shift through and select the right client base and while tackling all these, identify new areas of possible growth. Develop resources at hand and work with all that is available to achieve maximum potential outcome. It is addressing issues with suppliers and sequencing. Project management helps in identifying the best venue to manage a process successfully.

Teamwork is part of the organization's 'software'. It is what makes the organization be its distinct self and what makes a difference. Are all McDonald's the same? Well, yes, but no. McDonald's was designed for all to be the same, but it does not work this way. All offer the same (pretty much) menu and there are clear expectations as to what one gets from any of them. However, each McDonald's is different because of the level of service one gets from one versus another. In one the bathrooms are a little cleaner, the smiles are more genuine and the operation works much smoother. This is what we are talking about connecting what is 'the most important resource', as one client CEO said once: 'It is the people and how they work together that makes the difference'. I remember we were standing at the parking lot at the end of the day and we saw some employees leaving the building so he turned and said: "Do you see these people leaving the office? This is the most important resource I have in my organization. All the rest I can replace at any time, but not this". This is no different than what Mr. Carnegie said as well. It stuck because this is exactly what distinguishes a successful organization - its people.

It is people and teamwork which help transform the organization moving it from where it is today to what it wants to become.

Teamwork helps create and foster the appropriate corporate culture, distinct in each organization. The connecting glue or corporate culture is the signature of each and every organization. It is unique, needs to be fed so it grows, needs to be fostered and protected. It directly affects Operations which leads to the next component.

Operations is all that it takes to get things done in an organization. The customer does not see the whole operation; it only sees the final product. Think of a swan; when you see it in a lake it brings in your eyes a very serene beautiful image. However, you do not see how hard it is pedaling under the water, you do not see how it turns and maneuvers and how it shifts from one direction to another. You do not realize the signals that it interprets as to the depth of the water, what is happening underneath, as well as to what is happening on top of the water, other flying creatures or the ones which are swimming next to it. We only see the regal presence of the swan and how it moves. This is exactly what is happening with your client. Your customer sees the package of service that your product provides which includes the product, its quality, quantity, delivery, condition, price, value, satisfaction, perception of success, beauty, fulfillment, need, to name a few. The customers only know that they want it at the right time, the right quality, the right quantity, the right price and at the right place. That's all! It might be simple for the customer, but consider what it takes to get this done. This is 'the swan' at work.

And all of that with the realization that if any of the above is not right, we just lost a customer!

So, what does it take to get the package of service ready for the customer? A series of activities which make what 'we touch' valuable. We are part of a supply chain whereby we get supplies to transform them into a series of combination of products and services that we sell to our customers. The operations can be classified into two types of activities, core and support activities. Some refer to them as profit and cost centers since ones are generating profits and the others do not.

Core activities are the ones that we can not do without. These are the most important ones, like: How and what do we do with new business. How do they show up to our doorstep? How do we select them? How do we process them? The second is the actual operations process itself. This is our own trade secret. The special touch and unique ingredient which makes our products and services such that the customer wants it. This is our secret formula that distinguishes our product from that of the competitors. The third is the final presentation of getting it to the client; the customer interface portion. This is making sure that the customer is happy and satisfied with the package of product and service. The fourth is the marketing presence in the market, creating and having an image that is what we want to portray to the customer and publics. Last, the fifth one, is all the after sales service support to the customer, knowing that the satisfaction of the product stays with the client way beyond the purchase moment.

The support activities include all the ones that we need to have to get the core ones completed. Namely, technology support, human resource, legal, procurement, etc.

In order to have the core activities/operations covered we need to have the right combination of people, knowledge, technology and daily approach to ensure that what we do is of the right quality and package that we want to bring to the customer. This entails the quest from sourcing the appropriate combination of material and equipment to the final disposal of the used product after the customer enjoys it. Don't forget we are responsible for the product and its packaging past the time that they are in the landfill. A quick example is with computers; all who buy one pay a disposable fee regardless whether there is ever intention of throwing it away.

Negotiation. Throughout the day, we negotiate: we negotiate our way through traffic on the way to work, we negotiate with our spouse as to what we will have for dinner, we negotiate with our employees and co-workers on salaries, time off, work issues, we negotiate with bankers, shareholders and suppliers. As soon as the phone starts ringing we negotiate with our customers for the rest of the day. It is the smoothing part of operations where understanding the politics and underline issues makes a significant difference.

It includes interpreting messages from the company's grapevine to dealing with bankers on available lines of credit and accounts receivable; it is dealing with irate customers or representatives from the capital markets. Understanding the mindset entails good preparation, while utilizing the best communication approach gives a better chance of success. The basis is correct communication, working towards the common goal. This is complemented with 'The more we do it, the better we become good at it'. It is a skill that we hone through experience, application and time.

Implementation is doing what needs to be done so that we can see products and services materialize into value for our customers which in turn generate sales and profit. It includes courses of action and planed installation. This is where plans are translated into actions that help produce products and services. All parts of the organization are synchronized to generate outcomes that will benefit the customer and in turn the organization itself. Phenomenal amount of work has been generated to ensure that Implementation is run smoothly, efficiently and effectively. Tools, methodologies and approaches are everywhere; from inventory tools to machine automation, from absenteeism reducing methodologies, motivation and reward schemes to customer review and satisfaction. Indeed a wide range of tools for every part of Implementation. The key is finding the ones that fit the circumstances the organization is in.

Outcomes are what the customer and society sees. Noone cares what it takes to get it done. Remembering that the customer forms opinions holistically, all aspects of an organization reflect outcomes. Service, product, material mix, communication, logo, contribution to society, lobbying, procedures, etc., are only but few of the areas for consideration.

We constantly compare ourselves with industry, peers and mainly: expectations. We measure outcomes for just about anything. Scientific methodologies which were introduced in the late 1800's led to measurement criteria which are applied in today's corporate analyses. Today organizations measure themselves based on the criteria they set themselves and whether they meet what they said they were going to meet. So, in addition to competing with the industry, "I am competing with myself". That is why organizations create performance outcomes for all activities in an organization. To assess whether they are attained and are in line with what they were meant to achieve.

We need to remember that we are as good as the very product or service we just sold. Remember: we live based on references. We are as good as the last reference we got from the previous client. We are as good as the last product we sold last. A happy client only talks to 3-4 people while an unhappy one talks to 7-9 people about the negative experience.

Urgent exemplifies what operations is all about. There is nothing in operations that can really wait since it directly affects output. Everything and everybody is on

Drive Your Business with Management and Certainty

a schedule to satisfy goals and outcomes. From the shareholders who constantly ask 'how much have you made for me in the last 6 seconds?', to the customers who demand 'state of the art' applications.

In the meantime, there is little to no room for mistakes. The customers may forgive you once (if they are strongly committed to you) but never twice...

So, fast, expedient, reliable, responses is the name of the game and we are standing in the middle of it orchestrating all actions.

9f

The Belt

The belt part of the business engine apparatus is management. Management depends on knowledge, ambition, skills as well application of tools to get things done.

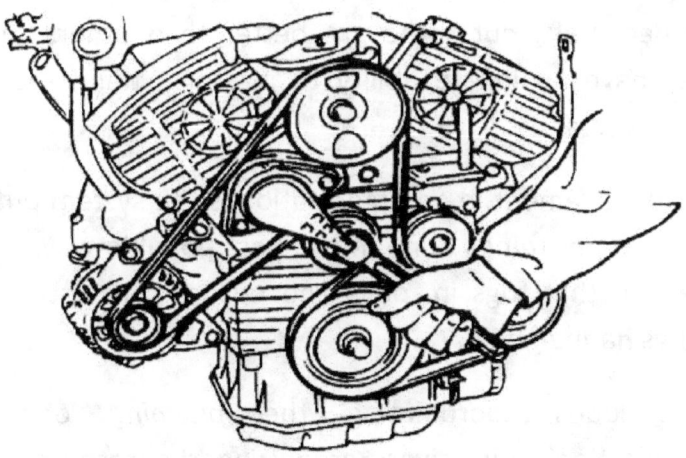

Source: http://www.justanswer.com/hyundai/6xixj-hyundai-sonota-change-serpentine-belt-sonata.html

Drive Your Business with Management and Certainty

Management is a learned art. Now, this is sensitive talk. You see, you can 'learn' art, but it does not mean that you can become an artist. On the other hand you can be an 'artist' without knowing much about art. It is the same with management. You can teach someone to be a manager, but it does not mean that they are good at it. It is like driving a car. We are all drivers, but how come some are better than others? These special ones, got training, experience, etc, etc, but they also have some innate ability making them good at it. This is the debate as to whether managers are born or made. Managers are made, but some are better than others because they have certain characteristics making them better than others.   The same like artists; art is a learned craft, but some are better than others since they have an innate ability to interpret things better than others.

So, management in an organization is the system put in place to get things done in the best possible way. It is the one that tugs in, pulls and pushes the system so things happen best.

It includes coordinating the *planning* of the organization's directives, *organizing* the resources to get what is needed done with the right kind of leadership of *human resources* and *overseeing* that what is supposed to happen happens.

In many cases we tend to ignore of the importance of the belt, for it looks as trivial, 'hidden', or underscored in relation to the car engine or other 'more important' engine parts. However, when there is belt failure then we find that the car can not run. The importance of the joint and interconnecting function of the belt becomes prevalent. If we fail at maintaining the functionality of the belt, we can not run the engine.

In business, the same belt failure situation might happen, directly affecting the organization's output.

When thinking of the belt system, we could draw 4 functional aspects of its mechanical and functional characteristics. These 4 aspects are Connectivity, Circulation, Balance, and Maintenance.

First of all, the Belt is used for connecting issues between the heterogeneous components. For example, it is used to interpret and install the appropriate strategy in operations. It connects the power engine of Strategy to the production of the goods and services. It serves as the controlling mechanism for procurement and process control and logistics needed.

Drive Your Business with Management and Certainty

Secondly, it works continuously, circulating without stopping during business operations. Like the blood system from the heart to the every part of the body, the continual circulation of the belt is the inevitable function for an alive business engine.

Thirdly, it works in accordance to the needs, speed, balance and tension needed to help the proper running and rotating operation. This is where TQM practices and ISO applications come in place.

In addition to each individual's, motivation, rewards, work-life balance we should also consider the balance between business and society. ISO 26000 deals directly with this concern: the organization's societal response.

Fourth, the belt should be maintained periodically the same as any other component. It needs to be lubricated, repaired or changed. It needs recognition, additional training, or replacement. All of the above considerations should be reexamined periodically to ensure better performance.

There is an enormous volume of knowledge on the history, functions and role of management and we will not spend much time on it other than to say that management is what makes things happen in an organization. Management is linked to getting things done.　Management is imbedded in every of the organization's operations.

Drive Your Business with Management and Certainty

9g

The Tentioner

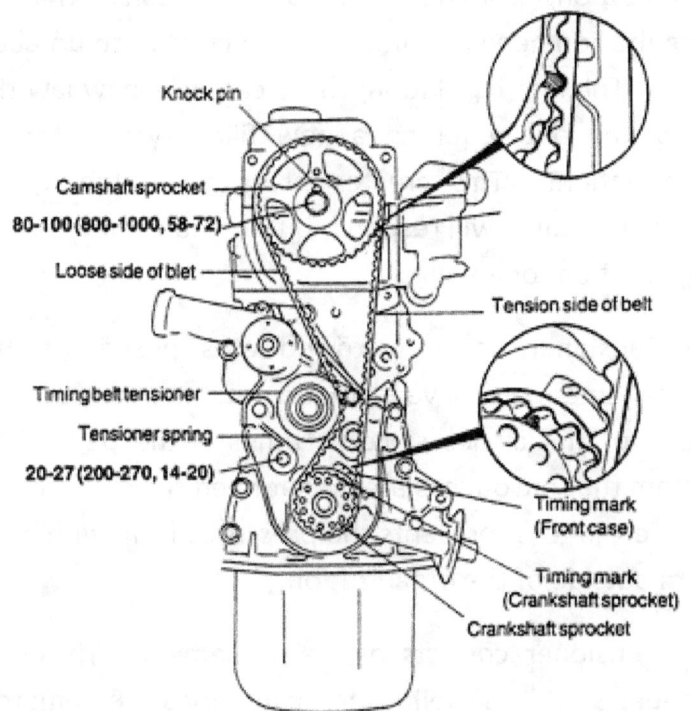

Source: http://www.justanswer.com/car/01f5k-put-timing-belt-2001-hundyia-accent.html

Drive Your Business with Management and Certainty

The Tentioner represents all the issues the organization faces from both the internal and external environments.

These issues range from payroll, to marketing, customer issues, government policies and competitors' moves as well as new technologies, currency exchange, political changes etc. In other words the Tentioner deals with all issues from within and from outside the organization, coming from all directions, that an organization needs to filter and select what to do about them. Think of legislation; there can be a new law that is coming out requiring a new filing system for the organization. This creates pressure to the system which, of course will respond, but it creates havoc in the organization for a while.

The Tensioner, as the word indicates, pushes the belt (management) to have slack or not. It also alters the speed of the circles since at times is the part of the system that introduces areas that need to be addressed. The Tensioner represents the pressures from within and from outside of the organization.

The Tensioner consists of many elements. These are grouped in the following categories: **P**arameters, **A**ccelerators, **R**eactors, and Key **P**erformance Indices.

Parameters are all and any of the issues themselves that an organization identifies (first), and chooses to do something about (second).

Notice – here we say that they are the ones the organization identifies because there might be some that we never know that they exist for a number of reasons: might not care to know all of what is happening, or we have not set up the appropriate method to collect the right information, or because we choose to disregard them because we do not want to deal with them due to resistance or being overwhelmed, just to name a few. More on this later.

Accelerators are the ones which would cause the parameters to increase the speed of needed response. Here we are talking about situations which need faster response than normal circumstances. Some examples might be that competitors are about to bring new products in the market or new technology innovation which might be replacing our existing one, or a political change in the system, new legislation etc. Another might be an emergency in our operations like an oil spill, product tampering, fire or other disaster causing immediate response.

Any and all of these events have a sense of urgency that needs to be addressed based on the impact that they have in the organization. Here we are introducing the sense of impact. That is the amount of potential damage that the identified external event will cause on our operations. The majority of the time an event will have an impact and consequences that we have to address and protect ourselves from.

Reactors are the mechanisms that an organization has in place to act, react and proact to make the overall organization function at its best. Here we are talking about knowledge that the organization gains as to how to apply a new system better, new computer program or new accounting procedure that helps the organization become better.

On the other hand, reactors can be events which are generated because of what the organization does: for example, sponsoring an event and based on the publicity gain a significant increase in the consumption of a certain product. Or, an actor chooses to use our product without our knowledge and we see increase in sales. These are events that we can not control, but at times influence.

Key **P**erformance Indices are the methods of comparison to find out how and what we are doing in comparison to the rest in the industry, sector, country, and the rest of the world. Remember; we are all

Drive Your Business with Management and Certainty

operating in one global economy and increasingly in one global industry. There is one global supply and demand for a product and services while there is regional distribution. The majority of the times we see ourselves as part of the regional component and not as the global part in it. As such we need to start thinking and acting as part of the larger picture, meaning that we need to interpret information from a larger pull of selected data.

Here we are talking about getting information about the competitors, suppliers and other groups which signify where we stand in comparison to them.

Drive Your Business with Management and Certainty

Drive Your Business with Management and Certainty

10

Gears and Transmission

Gears/transmission is the enhancing mechanism that managers should always keep in mind. It enables each manager to get better results with the normal input and effort by leveraging synergistic effects.

If there is no gears/transmission system in the engine apparatus, we have to put effort and input at same constant rate of each process while the output will have

Drive Your Business with Management and Certainty

uneven results. This is due to the fact that there are different output needs.

But if we could design and arrange the gears/transmission system into the business, we can save/reallocate efforts and inputs thus gaining more output out of the same effort. The productivity gains yield better and more output leading to more profitability and more output than what the customers would expect from the normal business activities.

Moreover, depending on the competitive situation and the turbulent fluctuating circumstances, we can use gears and transmission for the better cohesive fulfillment of customer requirement.

Changing Gears

To change gears is not easy since it takes significant amount of coordination, appropriate RPM and knowledge. Let alone the fact that all passengers should be ready for it. Sometimes the shifting is smooth and sometimes the gears grind and the car can even stall... it takes a significant amount of training and technique to master the art of smooth gear changing process. It varies on the car itself, terrain, circumstances, the driver, and the works.

This is when we are talking right sizing the organization in order to achieve better outcomes. This is when the organization's structure follows the strategy. It grows and contracts according to the degree of growth, expansion, and speed of growth.

This is when we are talking having the right transformation manager to take the organization to the 'next level'.

This is when we are talking about growing pains; this is when we are talking about having the right people on board as to where you want to be and not where you are now.

Change of Direction

As the leader and the owner of the business activity and its major process, you should change the organization's direction in accordance to the business and market reality.

There are 3 domains/zones, 3 uncertainties and 3 issues of change to keep in mind as the business owner and business activity-process owner. Let's call them the 3 DUIs.

The first DUI; the 3 Domains/zones are: company mission, goals/objectives, and strategies.

The second DUI; the 3 Uncertainties are: market, customer, and competitors.

The third DUI; the 3 Issues are: sales activities and returns (sales price and service, sales trends, and sales performance), operational quality (operations control or hazard management), and logistics.

When there are any signals, unexpected deviation, or early warning signals at any of the 3 DUIs, managers should decide when and what to change quickly.

The DUIs would send a message whether there is a need for organizational turnaround.

The turnaround could be Operational or Strategic. It requires a completely different approach and skill set for each one.

This is where knowledge and skill become imperative along with ability to detect which is the best way to achieve best outcome. It is whether you have the ability and knowledge:

- to use any of the knowledge, skill or organization's developed knowledge and Spare resources (spare tires),

- the degree of Depth of the needed transformation,

- of needed Skill level for the new organization and whether it already exists within the organization, or whether you need to acquire it,

- to change gears in the CEO's team and support within the organization so to not cause it to grind unnecessarily.

Drive Your Business with Management and Certainty

11

Tires: Operation – customer contact

Where the rubber meets the road.

It is the organization's operation the direct contact with clients. As in the car where there is a dashboard indication as to the tire's pressure, the same applies in the in the organization's dashboard equipment readout. The management office follows to identify wear and tear and any and all Personnel/operational issues.

There are winter tires, summer tires, truck tires, trailer, and race tires, performance, high or low profile tires, white wall or raised lettered ones. They have to match and need to be watched for even wear since they might indicate another issue with the car, like alignment, socks' wear or other issues.

When worn it should be replaced in a timely manner. Whatever the organization has a high performance engine or gears, it should be operated with the right set of tires – expertise, knowledge, skill level.

Drive Your Business with Management and Certainty

If the tires are worn out after the available period, it will be the most desirable case. But, sometimes tire failures could happen due to unexpected situations: the competitors' reactions, business circumstances, employees' failure or other hazard issues.

So we need to think of retreading the tire, or retraining the employees.

When a tire goes flat we need to find out if we have an unmotivated employee, and to act accordingly. Are we going to just put air in it, patch it, or replace it? This is where we need to have a clear understanding as to what it is that we are after so we can have the right interface at the marketplace.

Drive Your Business with Management and Certainty

Think how the tires act when they are not the right ones. When you have the winter tires, they are great in the winter, but in the summer, the run rough and they make a lot of noise. The same applies with the organization's employees: need to have the right kind for the right ride.

Remember what the hockey coach said: "it is not important as to where the puck is now. It is more important as to where the puck is going to be". So, we need to have the right kind of HR as to where we want the organization to be and for the employees to have the knowledge and depth of understanding of the size and complexity we want to achieve.

12

Trunk - Spared resources

The Spared resources can be tangible or intangible. They can be patents and new innovations, or the organization's image on the street; it can be the speed of new products in the market, or strength of the brand image.

http://www.hyundai.com/kr/index.do

The spare tire – ready to jump into work. The same applies with any of the spare resources. Kodak had a phenomenal amount of unutilized patents to the tune of more than 10,000 of them which became a commodity when the company went bankrupt. They also were the first to invent the digital cameras but the scraped it as a venture due to the fact that 'they were in the film business'. Sometimes, the spare resources could be used to your advantage and sometimes the driver becomes too cocky "know it all".

http://www.hankooktireusa.com/Main/default.aspx

The trunk is used for reserves of arbitrary purposes and for carrying materials, resources, tools or spare seats. For instance, if the engine room is filled with the energy transformative engine and other devices, the trunk might be used as a second engine room, electronic

Drive Your Business with Management and Certainty

devices or control units as well as information and knowledge sourcing room.

In addition to those usages, the trunk could be used as storage for spared resources in case of emergency.

The spare resources could include an emergency blanket, or the emergency kit in the truck of your car. This translates to the war room which the majority of the large organization have. In the war room the organization's representatives run different scenarios applying them in case of emergency. This is honing the skills and knowing what to do in undesirable situations. The best is when you have the war room and resources and you do not have to use it. This is the best case scenario.

At the same time one might have the spare tools, but does not know how to use them and what to do with them. Yes, you might have a spare tire, but when was the last time you changed one? This is when you might can roadside assistance to get it done for you. This is the same as hiring a consultant to do it for you.

This is where you might need a jack as support to change the tire.

This is when you might need water, life support in case of need. This is the line of credit that you might have as an organization, available in case of emergency.

All of these become part of the organization's ability to get things done and available resources for response.

13

Windshield - The View of World

Windshield is for view of anything on coming. It shields wind and dirt from outside and helps in navigating, judging and controlling driving activities. In addition, it enables for the driver to look and see what is happening at the front environment and situational reality.

The driver can see the signals and events during the business operations such as the reaction of the customers and market players as well as the road conditions, weather and the market traffic reality.

In looking outside the window the driver is constantly is performing an Environmental Scanning. Some of the information for the scan includes assessment of the internal conditions of the car/organization as we already talked about with the dashboard dials. However, the majority of the Environmental Scanning is directed outside the organization.

As part of looking into the future the driver is trying to see as far as one can possible see. In the process of scanning the driver uses all possible means to infer as to what will be happening in the future.

The driver of a car, does not only look at the car ahead, but the driver looks at the speed of flow, the next curve and whether there are any lanes which are busier than others; in addition, the driver is looking for the slow drivers, the big trucks, new entrances to the freeway, cops and anything in between. It is the same in business; the CEO and the team is looking at the competition, size, moves, new entrants in the market, government regulations. All of these signals are collected and interpreted so to make sense and decide as to when, how and what to respond.

Of course competition is of primary concern in addition to 'the rules of the road'. The rules represent the regulatory requirements. In addition, the driver(s) look for everything that occupies space in the freeway; from motorcycles, to big trucks, pedestrians or debris. The next concern is the rivalry, which is basically getting the best space in the lane you are in so that you are as far ahead as you want to be, with the speed and conditions you choose. All of these are in line with the organization's mission so to fulfill where it is that you want to be and how you get there.

Signals from the external environment is coming on to the organization containing certain information. Each signal is classified as an issue necessitating different response based on the type of information it contains. For instance, some issues might have a significant impact on the organization, which means that there is a need for an immediate response, while others might not be as impactful and not much is needed to be done.

Here is an example; while driving down the road, you might get a bug that will hit our windshield; you will not try to avoid it, other than your realizing that the next time you stop for gas you need to clean your windshield. However, if you see a kangaroo in front of the car, you will most definitely try to avoid it. If you hit it, there is high likelihood that you will be injured.

The same applies with all signals. A decided response is put in place for each of them. Depending on the strength of the signal it might necessitate an immediate response, or a delayed one. This is where the Real Time Response mechanism is put in place depending on the type of issue at hand.

Now, in addition to the windshield, we also have the side windows as well as the back windows.

The side windows we use them to assess how we are doing in relation to the competition and to assess how we are doing in comparison to the rest of the world. This is where industry comparison information becomes critical so to have an objective view of what is happening for comparison purposes.

In addition we have the back window which we also use to see how fast competitors are catching up with us. In addition, we use it to find out what has happened to us so to have a better idea of our performance.

Even though we drive forward we look backward to assess what has happened in the past and thus to assess what could happen in the future.

We also need to address the seating arrangements. Each seat has a better view of certain sides of the organization and the input of other passengers sometimes is needed for better navigation. For instance, the driver is asking the co pilot for directions, or the back seat passenger to help in parking, or to spot certain things. You see, all passengers contribute to the organization; some look in front, some to the side, some in the back, while others interpret information from the past and help to drive into the future. All passengers have the same goal in mind: to reach the destination intact, with a good spirit and with honed skills.

Of course there might be sometimes passengers who think that they are in a taxi, where someone else is driving it and they are there are there only for the ride. That might be good for a short while, but it cannot last for very long since all need to contribute a commensurate amount of effort.

Collecting and interpreting all of the information is a daunting task. The car is moving, things are happening, passengers are talking, internal information is also brought to attention and the driver is thirsty or hungry to name a few.

Based on the types of events, the degree of complexity of issues, discontinuity of occurrence and speed of change, the external Environment is classified in 5 levels of turbulence. Levels 1-3 are history driven environments, whereby one can extract information from the past and pretty much project what will be happening in the future. Levels 4 and 5 are future based environments where new information needs to be collected to decide what might be happening in the future.

The assessment of the level of turbulence is predominantly based on the correct triplet of: Collecting - Analyzing - Interpreting of signals.

That is why there can be a significant amount of varried response due to the fact that each company team could make different decisions based on slightly different information.

We would like to end by talking a little about cleaning the windshield and which helps Collect - Analyze - Interpret information correctly.

This is vital since it includes constantly honing new skills, being in tune with reality and consistently setting up a mechanism to filter information. This by itself is part of a skill set to be discussed later.

Drive Your Business with Management and Certainty

14

Ignition

When we talk about the ignition, lots of subjects might come to mind from the business and management perspective.

http://www.bestpartstore.co.uk/ignition-system/hyundai

To start we have basic questions on igniting the business, as to what causes a business to start, what is its purpose and who does what in igniting it. And then we are engaged in business on a daily basis. How different is with starting the car in the morning?

So, Ignition refers to 2 different things:

1. Ignition of the business itself, and

2. Ignition on a daily basis.

Let's talk about each one for a bit.

Ignition on a daily basis

When we start the engine in the morning, we just turn on the key without any thought, because everything is set to operate the car. Basic rpm has been set at around 8,000 and all other conditions such as fuel supply, temperature range, electricity, spark are in place. The only think that we, as drivers, need to think is where to go and which route we would take without any considerations of the automobile's operations.

The same applies in business. When we run the business, we have to set the basic conditions so that it will start. These basic conditions are the 9Cs. These are: business **C**omponents, **C**ontrol logic and systems, **C**onditions and constraints, **C**ompetition, **C**ustomers,

Drive Your Business with Management and Certainty

Circumstance, business **Cl**imate, **C**ommitment and **C**ompliance

Figure 6 illustrates the 9Cs. All of them have to be set and be in balance so that the engine will start and work in its optimum performance.

On a daily operation the 9Cs and daily goals need to be reset when igniting. This has to happen to reflect not only the external business targets, but also the internal components and at the same time counterbalancing all other Cs.

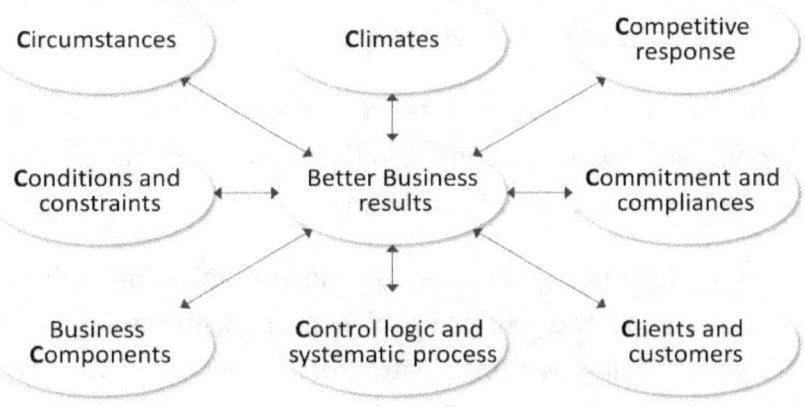

<Peter H. Antoniou and D. J. Park, 2013>

Figure 6: 9C Settings for the Better Business results

Ignition of the business itself

Drive Your Business with Management and Certainty

If we consider the venturing or creating a business, the ignition matters since it deals with entrepreneurial tasks.

In entrepreneurial context, ignition of business includes the basic motives in starting a business including its design and execution.

Sometimes it starts with the basic notion to earn money, to satisfy an unfulfilled need, or to solve a social issues problem.   Whichever the cause or the motive is, it requires an ignition mechanism to start a business.

When we talk about the 'entrepreneur' and 'enterprise', there is some confusion in understanding the concept and the meaning of these terms.

Normally, we use the term the enterprise as a big company by considering it with its scale. Some people use this for the private company as well.

Basically enterprise means the organization which responds to the issues, problems, or to something that needs coping within a situational environment.   An entrepreneur is the one who pursues the enterprise activities.

The prime subject of the enterprise or entrepreneur is coping with reality. (Scale or Scope follows next.)

Business Ignition comes from the enterprise/entrepreneurial purpose, which requires passion, purpose and performance.

Passion comes from business will and Intelligence; Purpose comes from personal will or causal motives; Performance comes from continuous development of the business.

So, even the shop owners open their shop doors with careful business settings and are well prepared to run their daily businesses. If they don't remind their basic passion, purpose and performance on the daily business execution and operations, they could not have the expected high business performance. They run their business just as normal even though the customers might want and expect different response.

In this case, the business ignition devices might not have the flexibly to cope with the situation. Those flexible ignition systems are very important to the markets which have seasonal trends or require rapid changes in the market place.

Now that we realize that Ignition plays a significant role in both the daily operations and in setting up new businesses, we'd better understand the ignition schema of the business execution process.

Figure 7 illustrates the Ignition schema as it relates to both the long term as well as the daily operations of a business.

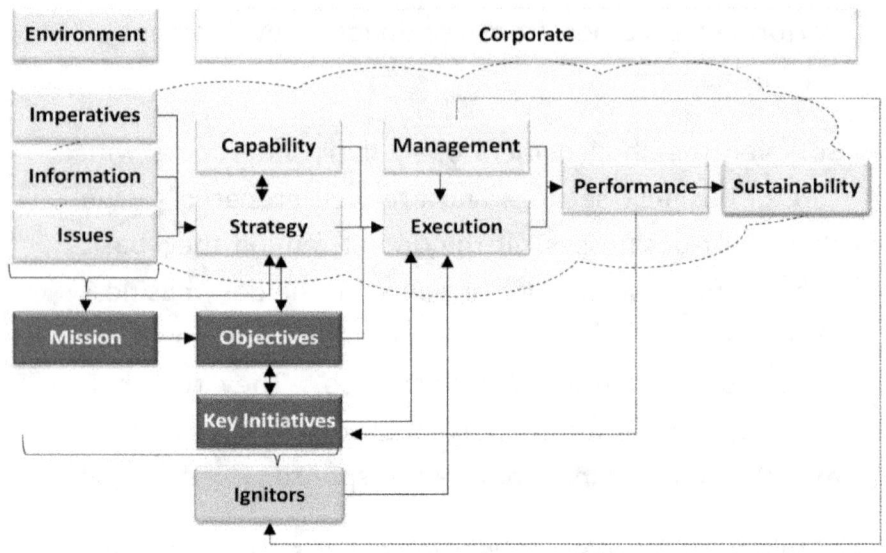

<Dong. J. Park and Peter H. Antoniou , 2013>

Figure 7: Ignition Schema of the Business Execution Process

At the bottom left side of figure 7, the ignitors are composed of 2 sets of parameters: Mission and Objectives.

Drive Your Business with Management and Certainty

Mission is directly affected by the environment and its imperatives, issues and information.

Mission is also directly affected by the organization's capability-strategy alignment. This alignment directly influences the organization's objectives.

The objectives come after the mission is formed as well as the capability-strategy alignment.

Management executes and ensures that the performance and sustainability is maintained.

In considering all of these aspects of the ignition scheme, managers often get lost in finding and selecting the ignitors in daily operations. When we drive the car, it is not difficult to find the ignition key hole. However, in the business reality, it is quite different to find the ignition key hole on a daily basis. It is a real big problem when a manager can not start the business engine when the other competitors already start to move.

In order to solve this situation, we have to set flags to help find easily "where we want to be". It is the same as in golf. The flag identifies "where we want to be". Usually it is called key flag. It might be an objective or goal to fulfill the mission or purpose, or it might be the

Drive Your Business with Management and Certainty

strategic initiatives to execute and implement the grand strategies.

If we could convert mission to the easily identified flag, it is easier to find where to go and where is the ignition key hole in daily business activities.

On the contrary, if we set the wrong initial key flag, what will happen? As you could figure out, we could not go, reach or accomplish the right goals, objectives, missions, so to speak, it would lead to failure even though we did our best and maximizing our best engine performance.

That's why the key flags are so important because they lead the daily business operational activities. At the same time, we might set very nice key flags, but it does not ensure that it would lead to action.

Case in point

A lady opened a hair salon. She was well educated and understood these concepts through her studies. So she set the key flags of the daily operation as the following ABC: Artistic, Beautiful, and Customer-first. She used these ABCs at every corner of the salon, and at every material, gowns, towels, brushes, memo pads and name cards. But she didn't know well how to actually perform those flags.

In this case, she had to draw and start the actual ignitors to accomplish the key flags. She had to provide the way and control the process to achieve the ABCs:

- For the flag of the Artistic, she needed to ask the hair dressers to study the current trends and what customers want.

- For the flag of the Beautiful, she hired a talented hair dressers or stylists and made them perform their expertise to the customers better every time.

- For the flag of the Customer-first, she created a customer participation program which allowed each customer to rate their session based on how satisfied they were with the service and the style overall.

So based on the rating results, the employees were rewarded periodically and they were motivated to do their best. With activities like these, the key flag of Customer-first was achieved.

These activities are called 'key initiatives' that will achieve key flags.

Don't forget this

Key flags and key initiatives when you ignite the business.

15

Fuel and others

In addition to the fundamental mechanism of the Ignition, we should emphasize the importance of the fuel and other external resources.

It is quite important to provide the fuel to the business. But, what is the fuel in business reality?

Some experts say that fuel, the dynamic force or power of business, is the willingness and the drive; some say it is the passion for excellence; and others support that it is the enthusiasm or entrepreneurial challenge to the society. All of these suggestions have a rational. All are correct since all have some components of what is needed.

The mental or philosophical motives are the generic fuel sources to get the business going.

However, we should not discount the economic and physical fuels which should be considered as well.

In addition to the fuel though, we strongly recommend the consideration of the combination of air supply and cooling devices to help run the car.

Most drivers focus on the throughput of the engine when they drive their car, but easily forget to check and control the external air or cooling systems.

The checking comes from job specifications. If a manager could accomplish the business engine throughputs, everything looks O.K., if not then there should be some engineering work to be performed with retraining, job enrichment, or restructuring (to name a few).

The manager should check and control the amount of the daily fuel usage, burn rate, as well as the compound of the external air supply and cooling system. These would help on the overall performance of the engine so it does not overheat and it has the maximum burn.

When we consider the performance review we have to look at the 5 external air supplies and 3 cooling devices.

Let's check the 5 external air supplies first.

1. Customers' comments and suggestions are the most important air supply to control and check the engine operations.

2. Competitors' information and market activities.

3. Market evaluation of our 4Ps (products, price, place, and promotion).

4. Regulatory information and market rules.

5. External governance suggestions and responses (business auditors, stakeholders, and investors).

Here are the 3 cooling devices.

1. Matching the speed with the controlling mechanism of the business and that of management.

   Need to control the turnover rate, or managing and control of the strategic investment.

2. Checking the performance measurement when it is out of line with capacity and capability.

   Need of balance in actions.

3. Monitoring the staff in daily operations. In particular, during daily and repetitive business operations. There can be conflicts and performance drops, due to repetition and lack of motivation.

Drive Your Business with Management and Certainty

Need for employee involvement and communication.

Drive Your Business with Management and Certainty

16

Using Maps For Navigation

In order to succeed driving your business, you need to have a map or a well loaded GPS.

You can have many kinds of maps to reach your goals, objectives or your mission as you like. However, we strongly suggest the 4 basic maps which are as follows:

1. The MCM(Money-Customer-Market) map

2. The Competition map

3. The Strategy map

4. The TIES (Techniques-Issues-Evaluation-Solution) map

More about the Basic 4 Maps

The first map is the MCM (Money-Customer-Market) map. Money follows Customers. So, it could be called the Money map, Customer map or Market map, since Money and Customers constitute the reality of the Marketplace.

The MCM Map

There are several checkpoints and logic for the design architectures of the MCM map. However the main key points are the volume, trends of growth, and the profitability in the Industrial-Market reality.

To understand it better we developed the 3 dimensional map as seen in figure 8. It helps check the direction you are driving the business. Every direction ranges from position Low to High. You can select any direction on this map.

Where do you want to head, it's totally up to you. You can select any direction from the Low to High on any dimension. However, every direction has its each combinations of Money (Economic value), Volume of Customers and Growth of Market.

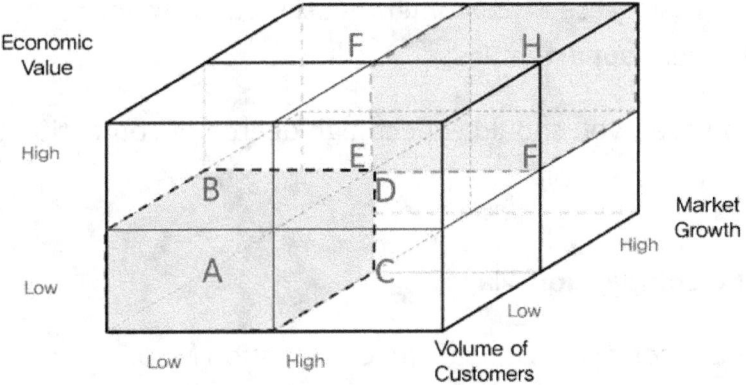

Figure 8: MCM Map

If you select the Low position in the above figure, you should expect low volume of customers, low economic value while the market growth rate is low. This means that you cannot expect high levels of profitability (with normal driving of your business) regardless as to whether you have prepared enough to run your operational successfully.

This business scene might look like a desert. If you want to get anything from this business areas, you should put extraordinary business efforts to get your goal.

On the contrary, if you head to H of the MCM map, you can get the high population of Customers, High economic value, and High Growth rate of Market. So,

Drive Your Business with Management and Certainty

you can access customers easily, and mobilize for business opportunities.

However, you should expect high degree of competition in the market place.

The Competition Map

The second basic map is the Competition Map.

It looks and operates in the same way as the previous one. However, the dimensions change. The dynamic dimensions for this map are the 3C reflecting the components of Competition.

The first C is composed from the **C**lassical strategic requirements:

- Capabilities such as Technology and Resource,

- Capacities, and

- Competencies, such as values of the organization, product distinctions and service operations.

The second C is composed from the **C**hampionship stake and rule of Game at the Market. Championship stake depends on the Market reality. If the Market stake is big, then you can expect strong competition including indirect competitive clusters as well as new ventures.

The Third C is **C**reation dynamics of the Market. Market dynamics of creation will drive out the old obsolete business, products and services.

The 3 dimensional competition map is illustrated in figure 9. It helps assess the competitive reality in driving your business.

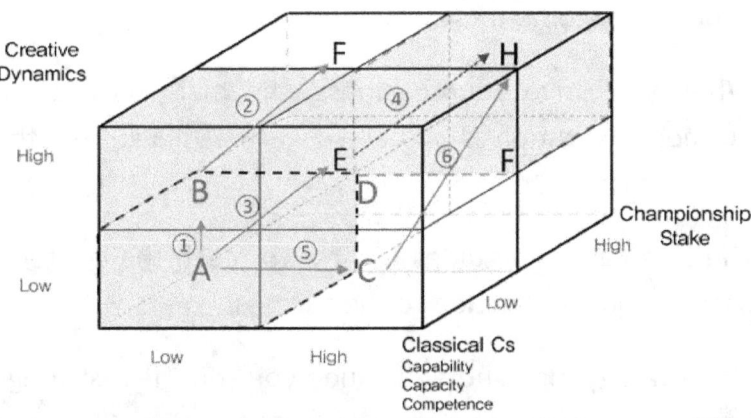

Figure 9: Competition Map

In following this map, you have to drive your business harder with extraordinary efforts and by using traditional ways to get your dreams.

Drive Your Business with Management and Certainty

It helps you to navigate through the choices of Competitive Environment and needed responses in equipping yourself and your operations.

The Strategy Map

Third map is the Strategy map.

The Strategy map was developed from the well-known SWOT matrix. The contextual logic of SWOT came from Igor Ansoff's Strategic success paradigm and strategic issues management.

When you drive your business, the main purpose of business execution is success. Figure 10 illustrates the SWOT matrix.

The Strategy map guides us how to reach the strategic path or course of action to the success.

The Strategy map should include your business strategy issues to respond to your business realities. Generally managers use the SWOT logic to start their strategic movement. However If you use the traditional SWOT matrix, not only some strategic issues are ignored, but also competitive measures might not be considered to

Drive Your Business with Management and Certainty

cope with your business reality. These kinds of problems come from the contextual design architecture of SWOT.

	SWOT Matrix	External	
		1. Opportunities	**2.** Threats
I **n** **t** **e** **r** **n** **a** **l**	**3.** Strengths	SO	ST
	4. Weaknesses	WO	WT

Figure 10: SWOT Matrix

This is why we developed the NSWOT to address the weaknesses of the classical SWOT matrix. Figure 11 illustrates the New SWOT.

Drive Your Business with Management and Certainty

SWOT Matrix		External		
		1. Opportunities	5. Needs of Customers, Market Trends	2. Threats
Internal	3. Strengths	SO	SN	ST
	4. Weaknesses	WO	WN	WT

Figure 11: SNWOT Matrix (SWOT-N Matrix)

It includes another column to address the identification of needs as they affect each of the SWOT components.

The main drawback of the classical SWOT is the identification of the points to enter in each of the categories in regards to the weight of significance of each one of them.

For starters, it is not easy to find which are the strong and weak points while performing self-diagnosis. This kind of self evaluation with relativism or subjectivism could lead to wrong direction of business execution.

Strong points lead us to self-conceit, weak points depress us to get over our basic shortcomings.

The most important thing in developing the strategy, it is not necessarily what we are or what we have, but what we really want to become and where do we want to be. Think about the Greek wars (Spartan and the Great Alexander) with Persian Forces.

In order to address the degree of effort needed to achieve what we want, we expanded the NSWOT with another attribute and called it SWOT-NE. The SWOT-NE is illustrated in figure 12.

In the middle column and row you can add necessary issues and efforts in considering for the successful response to the business reality. You can also add risk factors, or competitors issues in this column.

With this matrix, you can select what you should do first and to when to do it.

Drive Your Business with Management and Certainty

SWOT Matrix		External		
		1. Opportunities	5. Needs of Customers, Market Trends, Competitors Issues	2. Threats
Internal	3. Strengths	SO	SN	ST
	6. Efforts to be exerted	EO	EN	ET
	4. Weaknesses	WO	WN	WT

Figure 12: SNWOT Matrix (SWOT-NE Matrix)

The TIES Map

The 4th map is the TIES (Technique of Issues Evaluation and Solution) map.

The TIES map is designed to prepare and deal with issues within your business.

When we plan what should be done, we sometimes might forget to keep in the forefront all what need to happen and we only deal with issues which are right in front of us.

Since there are a lot of issues to address and most of them are overlapping, it can become quite difficult and complicated to address each of them.

In order to articulate these issues, respond successfully and be well prepared you can use the TIES map.

The TIES map helps in diagnosing what should be done, and to follow for successful execution.

The TIES map uses the right and left hand concept whereby the left hands is for thinking and the right hand is for doing.

Figure 13 illustrates the left hand naming the fingers from the thumb, as Main, Causal, Relational, Overall, and Urgent figure to think what are the issues or things to be done during the predestined, or planning period. And be careful to pick the third finger to check the relational concerns.

1. What is the main, core issue?

2. What is the causalities of the issues?

3. What is the related phenomena or issues?

4. What is required as the overall response?

5. What is required as the urgent response?

Figure 13: Left Hand Thinking Principle

1. What are the main, major or core response?

2. What are the causal responses?

3. What are the relational responses?

4. What are the overall responses?

5. What are the urgent responses?

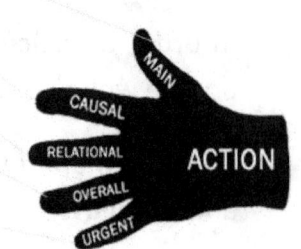

Figure 14: Right Hand Action Principle

In the same way figure 14 illustrates the right hand naming the fingers from the thumb, as Main, Causal, Relational, Overall, and Urgent.

The fingers are in sink and in line with the first hand thinking conclusions as to what should be done during the planning period. Do not forget to pay attention to the third finger in order to check the relational concerns.

The summary of the issues identifies by using the left and right hand analysis are entered into the TIES map illustrated in Figure 15.

I. Diagnosis of the Strategic Issues			II. Solution and response of the Strategic Issues		
Cause • •	Overall Strategic Issues		Overall Strategic Response	Causal Response • •	
Main issues • •				Main (Major) response • •	
Related phenomena •	Urgent issues		Urgent Response	Relational response • •	

Figure 15: TIES map of Thinking and Action Principle

In checking the left and right sides of the TIES Map, you can find what is left to be solved. In addition, you can add new issues during driving your own business to success.

Check your maps periodically

Unfortunately you cannot buy these 4 maps at a gas station or shops. But don't worry, if you didn't have these maps until now, you can draw them and use them for your navigation.

These maps need to be updated with the map navigation data, so you do not miss your path. So check and update them. These are your GPS for your business success.

When the path lost

When you forgot, or lost the path in your business, don't panic. You can exit the current route/approach, and rethink with the use of the 4 maps your path and direction.

If your business performance is not satisfactory, or there are some problems in your business, find the way with studying what the winners did in those situations; benchmark. Learn from others, not only competitors but also from the every source of media, institutions and specialists. Open your ears, eyes and minds. You can find the way, path in your maps.

Do not underestimate your efforts and intelligence. You are already the champion from start. You already have full capability of your own efforts and intelligence. By knowing and realizing this, you can design and develop your own success strategy in your life.

"If you can conceive it, you can achieve it"

The authors realized that the capability or competency of business persons is a significant matter when one exerts his/her best efforts and intelligence in achieving success.

This our main finding and fact in achieving success during over a 20 years study and consulting experience.

Manage your business with facts, do not mislead your path and put your best effort forward in driving your business and life. That's our simple and final message.

Drive Your Business with Management and Certainty

Summary

One thing for certain is that all of these components co-exist in an organization, are interdependent and are grouped in a way that makes sense. Now, how can we move from where we are today to the next level? This is what makes the wheels turning.

We would like to end with Peter Drucker's three quotes:

"The best way to predict the future is to create it."
"The purpose of a business is to create a customer."
"Business has only two functions - marketing and innovation. All the rest are costs."

So, we would like to leave you with this final thought because the future is in our hands and we have the apparatus to make it work.

So, let's go for a spin.

Drive Your Business with Management and Certainty

References

Books worth reading

Philip Kotler, Hermawan Kartajaya, Iwan Setiawan, Marketing 3.0: From Products to Customers to the Human Spirit, Wiley, 2010

Peter F. Drucker, The Effective Executive: The Definitive Guide to Getting the Right Things Done, Harper Business, 2006.

Michael E. Porter, On Competition, Updated and Expanded Edition, Harvard Business School Press, 2008.

Gary Hamel, What Matters Now: How to Win in a World of Relentless Change, Ferocious Competition, and Unstoppable Innovation, Jossey-Bass, 2012.

Thomas J. Peters, The Little Big Things: 163 Ways to Pursue EXCELLENCE by, HarperBusiness, 2012.

Robert A. G. Monks and Nell Minow, Corporate Governance, Blackwell Publishing, 2004,

Drive Your Business with Management and Certainty

Jim Underwood, More Than a Pink Cadillac - Mary Kay Inc.'s Nine Leadership Keys to Success, McGraw-Hill Trade, 2002.

Eric Ries, The Lean Startup: How Today's Entrepreneurs Use Continuous Innovation to Create Radically Successful Businesses, Crown Business, 2011.

Richard Rumelt, Good Strategy Bad Strategy: The Difference and Why It Matters, 2011

Harvard Business School Press (Editor), Strategy: Create and Implement the Best Strategy for Your Business, 2005.

David Dranove, Sonia Marciano, Kellogg on Strategy: Concepts, Tools, and Frameworks for Practitioners, Wiley, 2005

Dave Ramsey, EntreLeadership: 20 Years of Practical Business Wisdom from the Trenches, Howard Books, 2011.

Jim Collins, Jerry I. Porras, Built to Last: Successful Habits of Visionary Companies, HarperBusiness, 2004.

30 Minute Expert Summaries, Good to Great ... in 30 Minutes - A Concise Summary of Jim Collins's Bestselling Book, Garamond Press, 2012.

Authors' introductions

Peter H. Antoniou, DBA, is Partner at Pomegranate International, a firm involved in *International Venturing*, *Educational* programs and *Consulting* activities in the Strategic Management area
www.pomegranateintl.com, drpha@aol.com

Dong Joon Park, Ph. D., is President of AIASM, a firm specializing in *Strategic Management* and *Enterprise Strategy Architecture*, *Educational* programs and *Consulting* activities

www.ansoffkorea.com,   nswot@naver.com

Drive Your Business with Management and Certainty

Other Books written by the Authors

Peter H. Antoniou, DBA

Strategy Format - Solutions for Ultimate Strategy

Korea   Soft   Strategic   Management   Research Institute, 2008

Management, Zen and I

US   Amazon - Booksurge 2007

Korea   ESPRO - 2008

US/Korea   Phone - Apple Appstore, 2010

The H. Igor Ansoff Anthology

US   Amazon - BookSurge, 2006

The Secrets of Strategic Management: The Ansoffian Approach

US   Amazon- BookSurge, 2005

               Adopted as a required text at:

Alliant University - graduate and undergraduate programs

CSU-San Bernardino - graduate program

CSU-Los Angeles - graduate program
CSU-San Marcos - undergraduate program
Mount St. Mary's College - graduate program
St. Leo University - graduate and undergraduate programs
Warnborough College, Canterbury, UK - graduate program

Intercultural Communication Skills
China   Sun Yat-Sen University Press, Guangzhou, 2004

Adopted as a required text at Guangdong University of Commerce and Law

Strategies for Developing Companies in Evolving Countries
Korea   Ansoff Associates Korea, e-book, 2003
China   People's University Press, Beijing, 2004

Business - Government Relations in a Global Market Place
Korea   Ansoff Associates Korea, e-book, 2003

Business Protocol for Professional Success in North America
Korea   Ansoff Associates Korea, e-book, 2003

Enterprise Marketing
Korea   Ansoff Associates Korea, e-book, 2003

Lexicon of Business Terms
Korea   Ansoff Associates Korea, e-book, 2003

Establishing and Developing a Business in the United States

China   People's University Press, Beijing, 2002

Strategic Management and the Relationship Between Government and Companies
China   People's University Press, Beijing, 2001

The U.S. Economy and the 21st Century's Trends
China   People's University Press, Beijing, 2001

Optimizing Profitability During the 21st Century
US   USICB at Alliant International University, San Diego, 2000
Adopted as a required text at the graduate program
Korea   Ansoff Associates Korea, e-book, 2003
US   XanEdu, 2003

A Guide to Select Colleges and Universities in the U.S. and Canada
China   People's University Press, Beijing, 1999

A Business Traveler's Guide to North America
China   People's University Press, Beijing, 1995

Negotiating with Americans
Greece   Paratiritis, Thessaloniki, 1995
China   Lanzhou University Press, Gansu, 1996
Korea   Soft Strategic Management, Seoul, 1999
Adopted as a required text at graduate programs in two Universities

Korea   Ansoff Associates Korea, e-book, 2003
Korea   Bandibuli, 2008
Korea   e-book - Kyobobooks.co.kr, 2013

Marketing - The American Approach to Business
China   Beijing Industrial Economic Technology Institute, Beijing, 1994

Competitiveness Through Strategic Success
Greece   Paratiritis, Thessaloniki, 1993
US   The Planning Forum, 1994
Korea   Ansoff Associates Korea, e-book, 2003

The Challenges and Rewards of Exporting to the United States
Bulgaria   CORPEX, Sofia, 1992
China   Xinhua Publishing Co., Jinan, Shandong, 1992
Greece Paratiritis, Thessaloniki, 1993

Dong Joon Park, Ph. D.

How to drive your strategy for start-up
Korea   Soft Strategic Management Research Institute, e-book, 2013

Enterprise Strategic Management: Enterprise Strategy Architecture and Strategic Governance
> Korea   Soft   Strategic   Management   Research Institute, 2011 (e-book, 2012)

Lead yourself Vol. 1. – Today's Success Principles: Fundamentals
> Korea   Soft   Strategic   Management   Research Institute, 2011 (e-book, 2012)

Lead yourself Vol. 2. – Today's Success Principles: Challenge

Lead yourself Vol. 3. – Tomorrow's Success Principles: Create your life
> Korea   Soft   Strategic   Management   Research Institute, e-book, 2012

Strategy Format - Solutions for Ultimate Strategy
> Korea   Soft   Strategic   Management   Research Institute, 2008

Management, Zen and I
> US   Amazon - Booksurge 2007
> Korea   Soft   Strategic   Management   Research Institute, 2008 (e-book, 2012)
> US/Korea   Phone - Apple Appstore, 2010

New SWOT Strategy 2.0 – Strategic Issues Solution Program

151

Korea   Soft   Strategic   Management   Research
          Institute, 2008 . (e-book, 2012)

Strategic Risk Management: Executive Techniques
Korea   Soft   Strategic   Management   Research
          Institute, 2008 . (e-book, 2012)

Success Strategy for Managers
Korea   Soft   Strategic   Management   Research
          Institute, 2008 . (e-book, 2012)

New SWOT Stratezy
Korea   Ansoff Korea, Soft Strategic Management
          Research Institute, 2005. (e-book, 2012)

Corporate Diseases: Is your company OK?
Korea   Soft   Strategic   Management   Research
          Institute, 1994, (e-book, 2012)

Soft Power Strategy
Korea   Sunglim,   1993,   (e-book,   Soft   Strategic
          Management Research Institute, 2013)
Japan   Toshibunkasha, Tokyo, 1993

**How to get your job: Strategy, Plan, Preparation, Approach
and Career Development**
Korea   Sunglim, 1992

Drive Your Business with Management and Certainty

No plan is to plan to fail: Strategic Management by Objectives

Korea Sunglim, 1992, (e-book, Soft Strategic Management Research Institute, 2012)

www.ingramcontent.com/pod-product-compliance
Lightning Source LLC
Chambersburg PA
CBHW072024190526
45166CB00015B/480

* 9 7 8 1 4 9 2 9 0 0 8 7 0 *